ENCOUNTERS WITH GOD

ENCOUNTERS WITH GOD

MICHELLE ANTOINETTE GARNER

ALL RIGHTS RESERVED SOLELY BY THE AUTHOR. THE AUTHOR GUARANTEES ALL CONTENT WRITTEN IN THIS BOOK ARE ORIGINAL AND DO NOT INFRINGE UPON THE LEGAL RIGHTS OF ANY OTHER PERSON OR WORK. NO PART OF THIS BOOK MAY BE REPRODUCED, IN ANY FORM OR BY ANY MEANS- ELECTRONIC OR MECHANICAL, INCLUDING PHOTOCOPYING, WITHOUT PERMISSION IN WRITING FROM THE AUTHOR.

UNLESS OTHERWISE INDICATED, ALL SCRIPTURE QUOTATIONS ARE TAKEN FROM THE KING JAMES VERSION OF THE BIBLE

COPYRIGHT@ 2024 BY MICHELLE ANTOINETTE

THIS BOOK IS DEDICATED TO THE LORD GOD OF HEAVEN

I WOULD NOT BE HERE, NOR BE ABLE TO WRITE THIS BOOK WITHOUT YOU. I THANK YOU HOLY SPIRIT FOR WORKING WITH ME AND TEACHING ME. THANK YOU HOLY SPIRIT FOR WALKING WITH ME THROUGH THIS JOURNEY.

YOUR SERVANT

MICHELLE ANTOINETTE GARNER

AS THE LORD HAS PLACED ON MY HEART TO WRITE THIS BOOK. I PRAY THAT THIS WILL MINISTER TO YOUR HEART. I PRAY THAT THIS WILL DRAW YOU NEAR. I PRAY THAT THIS BOOK WILL KINDLE A FIRE WITHIN YOU FOR THE TRUE AND LIVING GOD. THAT YOU WOULD WALK WORTHY OF HIM (I THESS 2:12). THAT YOU WOULD WALK WITH HIM IN SPIRIT AND IN THE TRUTH (JOHN 4:24). AND NOW IS WHEN THE TRUE WORSHIPPERS SHALL WORSHIP THE FATHER IN SPIRIT AND IN TRUTH, FOR THE FATHER SEEKETH SUCH TO WORSHIP HIM. GOD LONGS FOR US, TO SPEND TIME WITH US IN HIS PRESENCE.

HE LONGS FOR US TO SEEK HIS FACE AND NOT JUST HIS HAND. HE IS THE GOOD SHEPHARD AND HE WANTS NOTHING MORE THAN TO PREPARE US FOR THIS LIFE AND THE LIFE TO COME. SO WE WILL OVERCOME IN VICTORY, THAT WE MAY REIGN WITH CHRIST AND SEE HIM AS HE IS.

(I JOHN 3:2-3)

AMEN

TABLE OF CONTENTS

INTRODUCTION..................................PAGE 1
IRON SHARPENS IRON......................................PAGE 2
SEEKING THE FACE OF GOD..........................PAGE 3-4
STORY TIME..PAGE 5-6
PRAYER..PAGE 7
PRAYER JOURNAL..PAGE 8-9
ENOUNTER..PAGE 10-13
CREATING ATMOSPHERES............................PAGE 14-15
ENCOUNTER..PAGE 16-18
SEPERATE YOURSELF FROM SIN...................PAGE 19
ENTER INTO THE PRESENCE OF GOD...........PAGE 20-23
ENCOUNTER..PAGE 24
HOW TO PRAY.....................................PAGE 25-26
PRAYER..PAGE 27-28
PRAYER JOURNAL..PAGE 29-32
VOWING...PAGE 34
PRAYER..PAGE 35
ADDITIONAL JOURNAL PAGES.....................PAGE 36-38

THIS BOOK IS ABOUT ENCOUNTERS WITH THE LORD AND PRAYERS THAT WILL COVER YOUR LIVES. I PRAY THIS BOOK WILL BE A BLESSING TO YOU AND YOUR FAMILY.

THAT YOU WOULD SEEK THE FACE OF THE LORD WHILE HE IS NEAR. THE LORD DESIRES US AND LONGS FOR US TO BE IN HIS PRESENCE AND SPEAK TO US EACH AND EVERY DAY OF OUR LIVES. MAY THE BLESSING OF THE LORD THAT MAKETH RICH AND ADDS NO SORROW BE ADDED TO YOUR LIFE.

MAY THE LORD BLESS THEE, AND KEEP THEE; THE LORD MAKE HIS FACE SHINE UPON THEE, AND BE GRACIOUS UNTO THEE. THE LORD LIFT UP HIS COUNTENANCE UPON THEE AND GIVE THEE PEACE. (NUM 6:24-26).
IN THE NAME OF JESUS.

SHALOM

I WOULD LIKE TO GIVE ALL GLORY TO GOD FOR PLACING ON MY HEART TO WRITE THIS BOOK. I THANK HIM FOR USING ME TO BIRTH THIS BOOK AND SHARE MY EXPERIENCES WITH THE LORD.

I'D LIKE TO HONOR MY FRIEND GENEVA COUNTEE. SHE PAST AWAY AT A VERY YOUNG AGE BUT GLORY TO GOD SHE IS DEFINITELY IN THE PRESENCE OF THE LORD. A PRAYER WARRIOR, WORSHIPER, DAUGHTER, AND PROPHET. THE LORD HONORED ME BY ALLOWING ME TO CONNECT WITH HER AND BRING HER INTO THE KINGDOM OF GOD. HE DID MIGHTY WORKS IN AND THROUGH HER, WITH HER UNWAVERING FAITH IN GOD. SHE HAD FAITH THAT MOVED MOUNTAINS. GOD GIFTED HER WITH TWO BEAUTIFUL GIRLS, JOY MADISON-KEY AND GLORIA (GLORY) HARRIS.

WE WOULD FAST TOGETHER, PRAY TOGETHER AND SEEK THE FACE OF GOD TOGETHER. WHEN WE WOULD COME TOGETHER WE WOULD SHARE WITH EACH OTHER WHAT THE LORD HAD REVEALED TO US IN OUR TIME ALONE WITH GOD. WE WOULD SHARE THE WORD AND REVELATIONS THAT HOLY SPIRIT WOULD GIVE TO US.
I REMEMBER THE FIRST TIME I EXPERIENCED A QUICKENING BY HOLY SPIRIT AT THE SAME TIME.

GENEVA CAME OVER TO VISIT ME AND SHE ASKED ME WHY SHOULDN'T YOU WEAR THE CROSS WITH THE BODY OF CHRIST ON THE PENDANT AND I TOLD HER I DIDN'T KNOW. SHE SAID SOMEONE AT HER JOB TOLD HER THAT AND IMMEDIATELY, THE HOLY SPIRIT QUICKENED US AT THE SAME TIME AND WE BOTH WERE LIKE "BECAUSE HE ROSE AGAIN!" WE WERE FILLED WITH SUCH JOY AND LAUGHTER. IT WAS AMAZING. WE WERE BOTH SO YOUNG IN OUR WALK WITH CHRIST. WE WENT ON TO EXPERIENCE SO MANY OTHER SUPERNATURAL THINGS. FROM SEEING ANGELS WATCH US FROM ABOVE AS WE BROKE BREAD IN THE WORD OF GOD. THAT'S FOR ANOTHER TIME AND MAYBE ANOTHER BOOK, IF THE LORD SAYS THE SAME.

I LOVE YOU GENEVA, MY SISTER (IN CHRIST), MY FRIEND. I MISS YOU DEARLY.

UNTIL I SEE YOU AGAIN.

THERE WILL COME A TIME THAT YOU WILL NEED TO KNOW HOW TO ENTER INTO THE PRESENCE OF GOD FOR YOURSELF! WE MUST BE DILIGENT, WE MUST BE STEADFAST AND WE MUST BE UNMOVABLE. THESE ARE TRYING TIMES, NOT ONLY IN THIS WORLD BUT IN THE SPIRITUAL REALM AS WELL. HEAVEN IS WHAT OUR GOAL SHOULD BE, AND WILL BE WHEN WE FIX OUR EYES ON HIM. WHICH IS, AND WHICH WAS AND WHICH IS TO COME; THE ALMIGHTY. (REVELATION 1:8). ALL OF THESE THINGS THAT I WILL SHARE WITH YOU WILL BE HOLY SPIRIT INSPIRED. I WILL ONLY SHARE WHAT I WILL BE LEAD TO SHARE IN THIS BOOK, WHICH IS FOR A TIME TO COME AMEN. GOD, WHO IS OUR STRENGTH AND OUR REFUGE IS A VERY PRESENT HELP IN TROUBLE (PSALM 46:1). PREPARATION WILL BE CRUCIAL IN THIS HOUR. USE THE WORD OF THE LORD FOR EVERY ASPECT OF YOUR LIFE. COVER YOU AND YOUR FAMILY. COVER ANYTHING THAT IS IMPORTANT TO YOU IN THIS HOUR. PRAY OVER WHAT EVER YOU PUT IN YOUR BODY, WHERE EVER YOU GO AND WHERE YOU LAY YOUR HEAD. WE WILL BEGIN TO SEE THINGS WE'VE NEVER SEEN BEFORE AND YOUR MIND, YOUR HEART AND YOUR FAITH MUST NOT FAIL YOU IN THIS HOUR. THE LORD SAID WHEN THE SON OF MAN COME, WILL (SHALL) COME, WILL HE FIND FAITH? (LUKE 18:8)

WHEN YOU'RE SEEKING THE FACE OF GOD, YOU ARE LOOKING FOR HIS PRESENCE. WHEN YOU'RE SEEKING THE FACE OF GOD, YOUR LOOKING FOR HIM WHERE EVER HE MAY BE. SO WHAT THIS WILL LOOK LIKE IS, WHEN YOU ARE READING AND MEDITATING IN THE WORD OF GOD; YOU ARE LOOKING FOR WHERE HE IS IN THE WORD. IN MY WALK WITH CHRIST JESUS, I WOULD SEARCH FOR HIM. AS A DEER LOOKING FOR WATER, AS I NEEDED AIR. I WOULD READ, READ AND READ UNTIL I FOUND HIS PRESENCE ON THE LOGO'S OF GOD'S WORD. YOU WILL KNOW WHEN YOU HAVE FOUND HIM, HIS PRESENCE WILL GIVE LIFE TO THAT SCRIPTURE, YOUR SPIRIT MAN WILL FEEL A STRENGTH ON THE INSIDE OF YOU. WHAT YOU HAVE NOW IS THE RHEMA WORD OF GOD, WHICH IS THE LOGOS THAT GOD HAS BREATHED UPON IT AND IS ALIVE NOW.

YOU CAN USE THIS WITH WHATEVER YOUR DOING, SEEKING THE LORD THROUGH THE WORD OF GOD. SEEKING GOD THROUGH PRAYER AND SEEKING GOD THROUGH WORSHIP. SEEKING HIS FACE. "WHEN THOU SAIDST SEEK MY FACE, MY HEART SAID TO THEE; THY FACE LORD WILL I SEEK. (PSALM 27:8)

I REMEMBER WHEN I FIRST GOT SAVED AND THE LORD BEGAN TO PULL ME TO HIMSELF. I LITERALLY HEARD MY HEART, MY SPIRIT SPEAK THAT SCRIPTURE. IT WAS LIKE IT WAS MY HEARTS CRY. I LONGED FOR HIM, I THIRSTED FOR HIM, I RAN HARD AFTER HIM. THIS IS WHAT HE WANTS, THIS IS WHAT HE LONGS FOR, THIS IS WHAT HE REQUIRES. BE YE STEADFAST, UNMOVABLE, ALWAYS ABOUNDING IN THE WORK OF THE LORD. (I COR 15:58)
BE STEADFAST IN YOUR SEEKING OF THE FACE OF GOD. THE MORE THAT YOU SEEK HIM, THE MORE YOU WILL FIND HIM.

TO SEEK HIM TO THE POINT THAT HE VISITS YOU IS AMAZING AND SCARY AT THE SAME TIME. MY FIRST ENCOUNTER OR SHALL I SAY VISITATION FROM GOD HAD ME ON MY FACE AS A DEAD MAN. I COULD NOT STAY UPRIGHT IN HIS PRESENCE. I WAS ON MY KNEES AND IT WAS LIKE I WOULD FALL ON MY FACE AND WHEN I WOULD COME TO, IT WAS LIKE HE SAT ME UP ON MY KNEES AND I JUST COULDN'T STAND IT. AS HE BEGAN TO SPEAK, I COULDN'T EVEN STAY CONSCIOUS TO HEAR THE WORDS AS HE BEGAN TO SPEAK. THE ONLY WORDS TO THIS DAY I CAN RECALL WERE "HEAR ME WHEN I SAY", I FELL OVER AGAIN UNCONSCIOUS. ALL I KNOW IS THAT AS HE SPOKE OVER ABRAHAM "AND I WILL MAKE MY COVENANT BETWEEN ME AND THEE, AND WILL MULTIPLY THEE EXCEEDINGLY. AND ABRAM FELL ON HIS FACE: AND GOD TALKED WITH HIM, SAYING. AS FOR ME, BEHOLD MY COVENANT IS WITH THEE, AND THOU SHALT BE A FATHER OF MANY NATIONS." (GENESIS 17:2-4) THIS SCRIPTURE OF COURSE IS WHEN GOD CHANGED HIS NAME FROM ABRAM TO ABRAHAM.

THIS IS KIND OF HOW IT WAS FOR ME BUT JUST IN THOSE WORDS THAT I DID HEAR HAD SO MUCH POWER BEHIND THEM BECAUSE THE LORD SPOKE THEM TO ME. I KNOW THERE IS A PROMISE OVER MY LIFE, THOUGH MY FLESH MAY NOT KNOW IT ALL, MY SPIRIT MAN HEARD EVERY WORD.

STORY TIME

THE FIRST TIME I MET MY NIECE WAS AT THE AGE OF FOUR YEARS OLD. MY SISTER WAS STATIONED IN GERMANY AND THAT'S WHERE SHE WAS BORN. SO WHEN I FIRST LAID MY EYES ON HER,

WE WERE ABLE TO CONNECT AS IF I HAD KNOWN HER ALL MY LIFE. I WAS SENT ON ASSIGNMENT FOR HER AND I DIDN'T KNOW THAT AT THE TIME. HOLY SPIRIT PUT IT ON MY HEART TO BEGIN TO READ THE WORD TO HER. SHE WOULD COME HOME FROM SCHOOL AND SHE WOULD WATCH HER CARTOON'S AND THEN HER HOMEWORK. I WOULD PULL OUT MY BIBLE AND BEGIN TO READ TO HER, SHE WOULD JUST RUN AROUND JUST PAYING ME NO MIND. IT WAS A REFLECTION OF ME, BECAUSE I WASN'T REALLY WANTING TO READ, I WAS TIRED AND I JUST WASN'T INTO IT. SO I BEGAN FLIPPING THE PAGES OF THE BIBLE AND THEN THAT'S WHEN I FOUND WHERE THE LORD WAS FOR ME IN THAT MOMENT AND AS I BEGAN TO READ THE PAGES OF LIFE; I BEGAN TO FEEL THE PRESENCE OF GOD. SHE STOPPED RIGHT IN HER TRACTS AND SAT DOWN LAYING WITH HER HEAD IN HER HANDS. AS I READ AND AS THE LORD WAS MINISTERING TO ME THROUGH THE WORD, SHE COULD FEEL THE PRESENCE OF THE LORD AND SHE SAT SO STILL AND PAID ATTENTION.

STORY TIME

ONCE THE PRESENCE OF GOD LIFTED OFF OF ME, AND I FELT WHEN IT DID. SHE WAS RIGHT BACK AT IT, RUNNING AROUND. THAT'S WHEN IT DAWNED ON ME THAT SHE KNOWS THE PRESENCE OF GOD. ITS IN ALL OF US TO KNOW HIM. THE BIBLE SAYS THAT THE WHOLE EARTH WILL BE FILLED WITH THE GLORY OF GOD. EVERY LIVING THING KNOWS THE VOICE OF GOD. THE EARTH DISPLAY HIM, AND HIS GLORY. SPEAK THE WORD OF GOD IN ALL THINGS, YOUR SURROUNDINGS; THEY WILL THRIVE AND YOU WILL THRIVE. SPEAK THE WORD OVER YOUR CHILDREN, READ TO THEM WHILE THEY ARE IN THE WOMB. SPEAK IT OVER YOUR HUSBAND, HUSBANDS, SPEAK IT OVER YOUR WIVES. LEAVE IT PLAYING IN YOUR HOME WHILE YOUR AT WORK. FIGHT FOR AN ATMOSPHERE THAT IS FULL OF PEACE AND LOVE AND FULL OF LIGHT. THAT CAN ONLY BE FOUND IN CHRIST JESUS. I REMEMBER LEAVING THE WORD OF GOD PLAYING WHILE I WAS SLEEP AND I STARTED HAVING SUPER NATURAL ENCOUNTERS FROM THE LORD. THOUGH MY NATURAL MAN WAS SLEEP, MY SPIRIT MAN WAS STILL BEING FED AND HE WAS BECOMING STRONGER THAN EVER

FATHER GOD,

I PRAY THAT YOU WOULD LEAD THEM AND GUIDE THEM INTO ALL TRUTH. FATHER GOD I PRAY THAT YOU WOULD TEACH THEM HOW TO SURROUND THEIR FAMILY WITH YOUR LOVE AND YOUR PRESENCE. THAT THEY WOULD PRAY OVER THEIR HOMES AND KEEP YOUR WORD THAT'S ALIVE, QUICK AND POWERFUL IN THEIR HEARTS AND OVER THEM ALL THEIR DAYS. FATHER GOD I PRAY THAT YOU WOULD UPLIFT THEM AND STRENGTHEN THEM IN THEIR INNER MAN WITH MIGHT. I PRAY THAT YOU WOULD KEEP THEIR MINDS AND THEIR EYES ON YOU. KEEP THEIR HEARTS FULL WITH YOUR JOY AND YOUR PEACE. FATHER GOD BE A HEDGE ABOUT THEM AND THEIR LOVE ONES. KEEP THEM COVERED IN YOUR BLOOD JESUS. FIGHT AGAINST ANYTHING THAT WILL FIGHT AGAINST THEM IN JESUS NAME.

NOW PRAY AND TOUCH AND AGREE WITH THIS PRAYER BY WRITING YOUR PRAYER FOR YOU AND YOUR LOVED ONES IN JESUS MIGHTY NAME....

PRAYERS FOR YOUR LOVED ONES

I WOULD GO ON TO ENCOUNTER MORE OF GOD, MORE OF WALKING AND BEING LEAD, GUIDED BY THE HOLY SPIRIT. I WOULD LIKE TO TELL YOU OF THIS ENCOUNTER I HAD BACK IN 2016.

(STORY TIME)

I BEGAN TO HEAR OF THIS PROPHET(I WILL WITH HOLD HIS NAME) AND SAW HIM ON TBN FILLING IN FOR A PASTOR . I BOUGHT A TICKET TO GO TO THIS PROPHETIC ENCOUNTER, NOT KNOWING THAT THIS SAME PASTOR WOULD BE THERE. HE OFFERED ALL WHO WERE THERE TO COME TO HIS MEETING IN SOUTH CAROLINA AND I HAD ALWAYS WANTED TO GO AND HEAR HIM SPEAK AND EXPERIENCE THE PRESENCE OF GOD.

SO WE WENT AND HE BEGAN SPEAKING AND TEACHING ABOUT THE HOLY SPIRIT AND HIS RELATIONSHIP WITH HOLY SPIRIT. I HAD NEVER HEARD ANYONE SPEAK SO INTIMATELY ABOUT THE HOLY SPIRIT BEFORE. I MEAN, I COULD FEEL HIS LOVE FOR HIM AND IT MOVED ME WITH SUCH PASSION AND LOVE LIKE I HAD NEVER EXPERIENCED BEFORE. IT IGNITED SOMETHING IN ME THAT I COULD NO LONGER COULD CONTAIN.

PRAYERS FOR YOUR LOVED ONES

I BEGAN TO WEEP SO UNCONTROLLABLY AND IT WAS LIKE THE PERSON OF THE HOLY GHOST SHOWED UP. THE HOLY SPIRIT SHOWED UP AND JUST SAT ON ME, I COULD FEEL THE WARMTH OF HIS PRESENCE, THE PRESENCE OF HOLY SPIRIT. I COULD NOT STOP CRYING.

I REMEMBER THERE WAS A MAN SITTING NEXT TO ME BUT I WAS STANDING AND THE PRESENCE BEGAN TO LIFT. IT FELT AS IF THIS HUGE WARM BLANKET WAS BEING REMOVED FROM ME AND I BECAME AWARE THAT I WAS ALL ALONE AND UNCOVERED. SO AS I OPENED MY EYES AND I'M LIKE WHERE, WHAT, LIKE WHY ARE YOU LEAVING, LIFTING FROM ME.

I STARTED TO LOOK AROUND AND THIS MAN IS TOUCHING ME ON MY LEFT SIDE TRYING TO EXPERIENCE WHAT WAS BEING IMPARTED OR ALLOWED FOR ME TO EXPERIENCE. SO I MOVED OVER FOR HIM TO STOP TOUCHING ME AND IMMEDIATELY THE HOLY SPIRIT SAT RIGHT BACK ON ME AND THE BELOVED PRESENCE OF HIS SPIRIT BEGAN TO REST ON ME YET AGAIN.

MY HANDS WERE LIFTED AND I WAS IN SUCH AWE, SUCH AWE OF THE PRESENCE OF THE LORD. I DIDN'T KNOW THAT THIS KIND OF LOVE COULD EVEN EXIST. THIS KIND OF PASSION THAT I DIDN'T KNOW THAT I COULD HAVE; SUCH INTIMACY WITH HOLY SPIRIT. BEFORE, IN THOSE MOMENTS, THERE WAS NO THOUGHT OF ANYTHING ELSE BUT HIM. AGAIN, THIS MAN NEXT TO ME MUST OF TOUCHED ME AGAIN BECAUSE THE HOLY SPIRIT LIFTED AGAIN. SO I LOOKED, AND SURE ENOUGH THIS MAN IS DOING IT AGAIN, BUT IN SUCH A WAY I COULD NOT FEEL IT BUT HE WAS ILLEGALLY TRYING TO TAP INTO WHAT THE LORD WAS ALLOWING ME TO EXPERIENCE. SO I MOVED OVER AGAIN, AND AGAIN THE HOLY SPIRIT SAT ON ME AGAIN. THE MAN BEGINS UTTERING AFTER TOUCHING ME AGAIN AT THE PRESENCE OF GOD SITTING ON ME. THIS HAPPENS 3 TIMES, AFTER THAT I JUST SIT DOWN AND I AM STILL EXPERIENCING HIS WONDERFUL PRESENCE. THE MAN DOES IT ONE MORE TIME AND I SLIDE OVER AND PASTOR BEGINS (PROBABLY WAS ALREADY BUT I WASN'T HEARING WHAT HE WAS SAYING) MINISTERING.

WE LEAVE THE SERVICE AND I JUST DON'T FEEL THE SAME ANYMORE. THE FRIENDS THAT I AM THERE WITH WANT TO GO OUT TO EAT BUT I JUST WANT TO GO BACK TO MY HOTEL ROOM AND JUST BASK IN HIS PRESENCE BUT I DIDN'T DRIVE. I LEFT MY CAR AND RODE WITH THEM AND SO I GO ON TO THE EATING PLACE WITH MY FRIEND AND HER SON. HER SON CHOOSES THIS PLACE AND I AM LOOKING AROUND AS WE SAT AND I NOTICE SO MUCH DEMONIC STUFF AND I'M LOOKING AT THEM LIKE, WHY WOULD YOU CHOOSE THIS TYPE OF PLACE TO SIT AND EAT.

AS WE LEFT OUT, I CAN HEAR THESE DEMONS GROWLING, TRYING TO GET TO ME. I CAN HEAR, ALMOST LIKE THERE WAS THIS INVISIBLE SHIELD OR BUBBLE AROUND ME. I CAN HEAR THEM GROWL, I CAN HEAR THEM ANGRY BECAUSE THEY CAN'T GET ANY WHERE NEAR ME.

I CAN HEAR AND FEEL THEM HITTING UP AGAINST THIS INVISIBLE SHIELD. THE SOUND OF IT REMINDED ME OF THE MOVIE STAR WARS WHEN THEY ARE FIGHTING USING THOSE LIGHTSABERS, LITERALLY I CAN HEAR IT WITH EACH HIT AS THEY TRY TO PENETRATE PASSED THIS SHIELD (I DON'T KNOW WHAT TO CALL IT). MY HEART STARTS TO FEAR, BECAUSE MY EARS ARE HEARING THINGS I HAVE NEVER HEARD BEFORE. THOSE DEMONS HATED THAT I WAS WALKING IN THE PRESENCE OF GOD. I PUT MY MIND ON GOD AND CAST DOWN THAT FEAR.

I SHARE THIS ONLY FOR YOU TO KNOW THAT EVEN IN TODAY'S TIMES, THIS IS POSSIBLE IF GOD ALLOWS AND YOU FOLLOW THE LORD. I EXPERIENCED SOMETHING THAT I DIDN'T EVEN KNOW EXISTED. I SHARE THIS WITH YOU, NOW YOU KNOW THERE IS A PLACE; A SECRET PLACE THAT YOU CAN LIVE IN (PSALMS 91), THAT YOU CAN ABIDE IN WHERE NO EVIL CAN DWELL. WHERE NO EVIL CAN HARM OR TOUCH YOU OR EVEN COME NEAR YOU. WRITING AND SHARING THIS WITH YOU EVEN NOW IS BRINGING TO MY REMEMBRANCE THESE EXPERIENCES THAT I NEVER WANT TO FORGET, BUT WANT TO LIVE IN THE MOMENT WITH HIM, WALKING WITH HIM IN THE COOL OF THE DAY. YOU WERE MEANT FOR SO MUCH MORE IN THIS LIFE, ITS NOT TO JUST WORK AND MAKE MONEY TO FULFIL THE DESIRES OF THE FLESH. ITS TO HAVE A WALK WITH GOD THAT TRANSCENDS THIS LIFE AND PREPARES YOU TO LIVE IN THE NEXT, TO HEAR WELL DONE THY GOOD AND FAITHFUL SERVANT. (MAT 25:21)

THERE IS A PLACE IN GOD THAT YOU CAN GET TO WHERE YOU DON'T HAVE TO TOIL. YOU CAN ENTER INTO A PLACE IN THE SPIRIT, CREATE SUCH AN ATMOSPHERE; THAT ALL YOU HAVE TO DO IS SPEAK.

ALL YOU HAVE TO DO IS CALL IT OUT AND CALL IT FORTH. JESUS, WHEN HE WAS GOING TO MARY AND MARTHA TO CALL FORTH LAZARUS. HE WAITED, HE WAITED; HE ALSO WAITED UNTIL MARY'S AND MARTHA'S WORDS LINED UP BEFORE HE CALLED FORTH LAZARUS. HE PUT OUT MOCKERS, UNBELIEF AND DOUBT. JESUS MADE SURE THAT THE ATMOSPHERE WAS RIGHT! ONCE AN ATMOSPHERE IS CONDUCIVE, YOU CAN CALL WHAT YOU NEED. IF IT'S PEACE, IF IT'S JOY, IF IT'S LOVE THAT YOU NEED.

IF YOU ASK GOD FOR IT, THERE IS A SOUND THAT YOU WILL HEAR, THERE IS A SHIFT THAT YOU WILL FEEL AND IN THE SPIRIT YOU WILL KNOW WHEN TO SPEAK, YOU WILL HEAR IT AND YOUR SPIRIT MAN WILL HEAR THAT SOUND. THEN YOU BEGIN TO CALL IT OUT (PEACE OH GOD, JOY OH GOD, LOVE OH GOD) WHATEVER YOU NEED, GLORY TO GOD. IT WILL PERTAIN TO THE THINGS OF GOD. THE THINGS THAT YOUR SOUL NEEDS. THE THINGS THAT YOU LACK, THE THINGS THAT YOU ARE HONEST TO GOD ABOUT.

IN THIS ATMOSPHERE, DAILY I WOULD FEEL THE TAP ON MY SHOULDER, FROM THE HOLY SPIRIT WAKING ME UP, WAY BEFORE AN ALARM CLOCK WOULD GO OFF. ALL MOST TO SAY, COME SPEND TIME WITH ME. I WOULD GET UP AND SPEND TIME WITH HOLY SPIRIT. I WOULD LOOK THROUGH MY CLOSET WHEN IT WAS TIME TO START GETTING READY AND I WOULD HEAR, WEAR THAT; AND THAT'S WHAT I WOULD GRAB TO WEAR. WHILE I AM GRABBING THAT OUTFIT I WOULD HEAR, I WANT YOU TO FAST TODAY. I WOULD BE LIKE OKAY LORD, DON'T GET ME WRONG; THE FLESH WILL ALWAYS BE THE FLESH BUT THE MORE YOU AFFLICT YOUR FLESH THE LESS AND LESS IT WILL HAVE CONTROL OF YOU. IT'S A DAILY WALK OF MAKING CHOICES FOR THE WAY OF THE SPIRIT INSTEAD OF THE WAY OF THE FLESH.

ONE DAY I HAD RECEIVED NEWS THAT A LADY THAT I HAD KNEW WHEN I WAS IN MY TEENAGE YEARS HAD CANCER. I WILL NEVER FORGET HOW A HOLY INDIGNATION ROSE UP IN ME AND I SAID WITH A LOUD VOICE; "THE DEVIL IS A LIAR". I GOT A HOLD OF HER DAUGHTER AND SHE TOLD ME WHERE SHE WAS AND WHICH HOSPITAL. AS I HAD MADE UP IN MY HEART AND IN MY MIND TO DRIVE ALL THE WAY FROM NEW MEXICO TO DALLAS TO SEE ABOUT HER; I CONTACTED. MY FRIEND GENEVA.

GENEVA MET ME AND I KNEW THAT GOD WOULD MOVE MIRACULOUSLY ON HER BEHALF. I MET UP WITH GENEVA AT THE HOSPITAL ROOM AND SHE WAS VERY HAPPY TO SEE ME. I TOLD HER WHY I WAS THERE AND ASKED IF WE COULD PRAY FOR HER. AS I BEGAN TO PRAY FOR HER, I FELT THE HOLYGHOST IMMEDIATELY BEGAN TO MOVE.

AS WE PRAYED FOR HER, THE ATMOSPHERE CHANGED. IMMEDIATELY I COULD FEEL THAT GOD WAS MOVING FOR HER. AS WE BEGAN TO WORSHIP, THE PRESENCE OF THE LORD BEGAN TO REST ON HER IN THAT HOSPITAL BED. SHE BEGAN TO YELL HALLELUJAH. I COULD FEEL HER FAITH IGNITING. I COULD FEEL HER SHIFTING AS THE LORD WAS SHIFTING THE ATMOSPHERE IN THAT ROOM. IT FELT LIKE LIFE IN THAT ROOM. SHE BEGAN TO GRAB MY HAND AS I WAS WALKING ABOUT HER BED. SHE PLACED MY HAND WHERE IT WAS NOW AN OPEN WOUND. WHAT I THOUGHT WOULD BE ONE THING, THE LORD DID ANOTHER.

IT WAS SO POWERFUL! WE WERE ON ONE ACCORD, WITH ,CHILD LIKE FAITH AND WE WERE BOTH WORSHIPERS. GENEVA FOLLOWED MY LEAD, AS I FOLLOWED THE LEADING OF THE HOLY GHOST. WE LEFT THERE FULL IN THE FAITH, FULL ON HOW GOD MOVED FOR HER, HER COUNTENANCE WASN'T THE SAME. GOING THROUGH THIS TAUGHT ME ONE THING, NEVER HAVE IN YOUR MIND WHAT YOU THINK GOD WANTS TO DO IN A MATTER. I BELIEVED THAT SHE WOULD BE HEALED IN THE FLESH BUT IT WAS ACTUALLY PREPARATION TO ENTER INTO ETERNAL LIFE WITH GOD; WHICH IS THE ULTIMATE HEALING ONE COULD EVER RECEIVE.

IN THIS BOOK THE LORD WANTED ME TO SHARE THESE ENCOUNTERS I HAVE HAD AND MY RELATIONSHIP WITH HIM. THE WAY THAT HE TOOK ME, SOME JUST DIDN'T UNDERSTAND. THE LORD TOOK ME ON THIS JOURNEY LIKE HE DID ABRAHAM, TO FORSAKE WHAT HE KNEW, LEAVE HIS FATHER'S HOUSE AND THE LORD WOULD SHOW HIM THE PLACE HE WANTED HIM TO GO. THAT PLACE IS WHERE THE PROMISES OF GOD WOULD BE FOUND, WHERE THE PROMISES OF GOD WOULD OVER TAKE HIM AND HE WOULD BECOME THE FATHER OF MANY NATIONS.

WHO YOU ARE CONNECTED TOO MATTERS, WHERE YOU FELLOWSHIP AND THE HOUSE, THE COVERING YOU SIT UNDER MATTERS. WHAT IS ON THE MAN OF GOD'S LIFE WILL TRANSCEND DOWN TO YOU. IT MATTERS WHAT LIFE THEY ARE LIVING FROM OUT OF THE PULPIT, BECAUSE WITHOUT A GENUINE RELATIONSHIP WITH THE LORD; WHAT DO THEY TRULY HAVE TO GIVE YOU? ONLY JESUS HAS THE KEYS TO ETERNAL LIFE. THEY CAN NOT LEAD YOU TO ANYWHERE THEY DO NOT KNOW THE WAY OR HAVE EXPERIENCED FOR THEMSELVES. ONLY A MAN OR WOMAN OF GOD THAT SPENDS TIME WITH GOD AND GOD HAS GIVEN HIM ACCESS TO THE KINGDOM AND HAS PUT WEIGHT ON HIS WORDS. NOT ONLY IN HEAVEN BUT IN THE SPIRIT REALM, THE EARTH AND HAS HEAVEN BACKING HIM WHEN HE SPEAKS. HE HAS ANGELS ON ASSIGNMENT HELPING HIM DO WHAT THE LORD HAS CALLED HIM TO DO.

DAVID, ABRAHAM, ELIJAH, ELISHA, ALL THE APOSTLES AND PROPHETS. TOO MANY TO NAME THEM ALL BUT THEY DID SIGNS, WONDERS AND MIRACLES AND IT FOLLOWED THEM WHEREEVER THEY WENT, BECAUSE GOD WAS WITH THEM.

I WAS IN A PLACE SPIRITUALLY, THAT THE LORD SO GRACIOUSLY ALLOWED ME ACCESS. BECAUSE OF THE COVERING I SAT UNDER, APOSTLE E.S. GRAY (MORE EXCELLENT WAY CHURCH) IN FORT WORTH, TX AND THE GRACE THAT WAS UPON HIS LIFE FLOWED OVER MY LIFE. THERE WAS A GRACE FOR ME TO ENTER INTO THESE PLACES IN THE SPIRIT. I WASN'T JUST A MEMBER, BUT A DISCIPLE. I WALKED IN THE SPIRIT AND WAS USED FOR THE KINGDOM OF GOD. NOW ITS NOT TO MAKE ANYONE AN IDOL, FOR THEY ARE MERE MEN; BUT THERE SHOULD BE HONOR WHERE HONOR IS DUE.

I AM GRATEFUL THAT THE LORD SAW FIT TO BIRTH ME IN THE SPIRIT UNDER AN APOSTOLIC MINISTRY, OUT OF AN APOSTOLIC ANOINTING. IT TRULY FLOWED FROM THE HEAD DOWN TO THE BODY AND IF YOU WERE HUNGRY FOR GOD, YOU WERE FEED. IT CHANGED MY LIFE FOREVER. SEEING ANGELS OFTEN, ANGELS COMING TO MY AIDE. HAVING AN ENCOUNTER WITH MICHAEL THE ARCHANGEL, THE CAPTAIN OF THE HOST COME TO MY AIDE AND WARRED ON MY BEHALF. KNOWING THIS AND EXPERIENCING THIS HAS GIVEN ME SUCH ASSURANCE THAT THE LORD OF HOST WILL FIGHT FOR ME IN EVERY AREA OF MY LIFE. THE LORD IS PLENTEOUS IN MERCY, PLENTY IN JUSTICE; HE WILL NOT AFFLICT. (JOB 37:23). HE IS SO MERCIFUL AND YOU CAN FIND GRACE TO HELP IN TIME OF NEED. (HEBREWS 4:16)

THERE IS SO MUCH THAT MATTER, PLEASE DON'T TAKE THIS LIGHTLY! IT MATTERS, I CAN'T STRESS THIS ENOUGH. WE HAVE TO SEPARATE OURSELVES FROM SIN AND OUR SIN NATURE. YOU WANT THE WORD OF THE LORD TO BECOME FLESH AND REAL IN YOUR LIFE. ALLOW HIM TO LET THE WORD OF GOD BE THAT TWO EDGE SWORD THAT IS QUICK AND POWERFUL AND SHARPER THAN ANY TWO EDGED SWORD; PIERCING EVEN TO THE DIVIDING ASUNDER OF SOUL AND SPIRIT. THERE HAS TO BE A DIVIDING OF THE SOUL AND SPIRIT. A GREAT BOOK TO READ ALONG WITH THE BIBLE OF COURSE IS CALLED "THE SPIRITUAL MAN" AND "THE BREAKING OF THE OUTER MAN AND THE RELEASE OF THE SPIRIT" BY WATCHMAN NEE. THIS WAS MY FIRST BOOK (ENCOURAGED TO READ) AT MORE EXCELLENT WAY.

IF YOU DO NOT HAVE A GOOD CHURCH HOME AND YOU WILL NEED ONE IN THE TIMES TO COME. PRAY AND ASK THE SPIRIT OF GOD WHERE HE WANTS YOU TO GO, TO BE TAUGHT THE WAYS OF GOD. HOWBEIT WHEN HE, THE SPIRIT OF TRUTH, IS COME, HE WILL GUIDE YOU INTO ALL TRUTH. (JOHN 16:13).

BUILDING A LIFESTYLE OF PRAYER IS CRUCIAL TO NOT ONLY YOUR WALK IN CHRIST BUT FOR OTHERS AND ALSO FOR STRENGTH IN YOUR SPIRIT MAN. (EPHESIANS 3:16). WITH PRAYER YOU WILL SEEK GOD. YOU WILL REPENT FOR YOUR SINS, COMMITTED, NOT REALIZED SINS (YOUR THOUGHT LIFE CAN CAUSE SIN) YOU BEGAN TO ASK THE LORD TO COME NIGH (NEAR) YOU. CONFESS YOUR NEED FOR HIM, YOUR DESPERATION FOR HIM. GOD ALREADY KNOWS THESE THINGS, BUT THIS IS YOUR WAY OF SANCTIFYING THE LORD AS GOD. THIS IS HOW YOU ACKNOWLEDGE TO HIM THAT HE IS GOD AND THERE IS NONE OTHER BESIDES HIM. THIS IS HOW YOU HUMBLE YOURSELF BEFORE THE ALMIGHTY. YOU CONFESS, YOU HUMBLE, YOU DECLARE YOUR DEPENDENCY ON HIM. THEN AS YOU BEGAN TO POUR OUT YOUR HEART BEFORE THE LORD, AS YOU ARE TOUCHING HIS HEART; HE WILL BEGIN TO TOUCH YOURS. YOU WILL BEGIN TO FEEL HIS PRESENCE, YOU WILL BEGIN TO FEEL HIS TOUCH. YOU WILL BEGAN TO FEEL HIM PULL FOR MORE OF YOU, WHERE YOU ARE. IF WHAT YOU ARE SAYING AND DOING YOU MEAN WITH ALL OF YOUR HEART; HE WILL RESPOND.

LET US HOLD FAST THE PROFESSION OF OUR FAITH WITHOUT WAVERING. (HEBREWS 10:23).

WE SERVE A GOD THAT IS LIVING AND BREATHING, GIVING US BOLDNESS TO ENTER INTO THE HOLIEST BY THE BLOOD OF JESUS, BY A NEW AND LIVING WAY, WHICH HE HATH CONSECRATED FOR US, THROUGH THE VEIL. (HEBREWS 10: 19-20). I KNOW, IT SEEMS LIKE A CONTRADICTION DOESN'T IT? FIRST REPENTING, THEN HUMBLE YOURSELF AND CRY OUT ASKING FOR HIS FORGIVENESS BUT THAT IS EXACTLY WHERE HIS POWER LIES. IN WEAKNESS BUT IN POWER. IN HUMILITY BUT IN BOLDNESS. THIS THING IS FULL OF TYPES AND SHADOWS. FORETELLING OF WHAT WAS, TELLING OF WHAT IS AND TELLING OF WHAT IS TO COME. THAT WE MAY KNOW HIM, KNOW WHAT WE WILL BE WALKING INTO WITH HIM. HIS PROMISES, WHICH ARE YES AND AMEN. LIKE TELLING A STORY, YOU MAY NOT HAVE OR GET ALL OF THE PIECES ALL AT ONCE BUT YOU WILL KNOW HIM AND WHO HE IS; YOU WILL KNOW HIS HEART, HIS MIND AND CHARACTER. THIS IS WHAT IT'S ALL ABOUT! THIS STORY, THIS LIFE IS ABOUT JESUS CHRIST.

HIS REVEALING, WHAT HE DID ON THE CROSS AT CALVARY. WHAT WAS PREDESTINED BEFORE US, BEFORE WE WERE FORMED IN OUR MOTHER'S WOMB. HIS LOVE FOR US, TELLS US A STORY. THE BEST LOVE STORY THAT STILL HASN'T BEEN COMPLETELY REVEALED TO US. IT'S STILL A MYSTERY BUT WE MUST WALK WITH HIM ALL THE WAY, WE MUST UNITE WITH HIM, BE LOYAL TO HIM THAT IN THE END WE CAN ABIDE WITH HIM FOREVER

SO WE HAVE BEEN TALKING ABOUT PRAYER AND REPENTANCE, WHICH IS A GOOD WAY TO LIVE YOUR LIFE BEFORE THE LORD. REMEMBER JOB " THAT MAN WAS PERFECT AND UPRIGHT, AND ONE THAT FEARED GOD, AND ESCHEWED EVIL". (JOB 1:1) " AND IT WAS SO, WHEN THE DAYS OF THEIR FEASTING WERE GONE ABOUT, THAT JOB SENT AND SANCTIFIED THEM, AND ROSE UP EARLY IN THE MORNING, AND OFFERED BURNT OFFERINGS ACCORDING TO THE NUMBER OF THEM ALL: FOR JOB SAID, IT MAY BE THAT MY SONS HAVE SINNED AND CURSED GOD IN THEIR HEARTS. THUS DID JOB CONTINUALLY." (JOB 1:4-5). SO YOU SEE, IF YOU READ JOB OR KNOW THE STORY; HE CONTINUALLY MADE BURNT OFFERINGS BEFORE THE LORD. NOW BECAUSE OF WHAT WAS DONE ON CALVARY THROUGH JESUS CHRIST, WE NO LONGER HAVE TO DO BURNT OFFERINGS, BUT THERE IS STILL A NEED FOR REPENTANCE FOR SIN WE SOMETIMES DO THROUGH THE FLESH. THERE IS NOTHING GOOD IN THIS FLESH (ROMANS 7:18)

LIVING THIS WAY BEFORE THE LORD BRINGS SO MUCH JOY IN OUR LIVES AND IT PLEASES THE LORD. IT BRINGS THE PEACE OF GOD, BEING IN HIS PRESENCE BRINGS HEALING AND WHOLENESS AND A LOVE THAT YOU'VE NEVER KNOWN. YOU KNOW YOU HAVE BEEN SEARCHING FOR IT, LOOKING FOR IT BUT TO EXPERIENCE IT HERE AND NOW, HE WILL LITERALLY MEET YOU RIGHT WHERE YOU ARE! WHEREVER YOUR LIFE SEEMS TO BE IN THIS TIME AND IN THIS HOUR, HE HAS A PLAN AND A PURPOSE FOR YOUR LIFE. WHERE IT'S BEEN CHAOTIC AND THINGS SEEM TO NOT BE GOING THE WAY YOU WOULD LIKE FOR THEM TO GO. SOMETIMES IT IS TO DISRUPT YOUR LIFE TO GET YOUR ATTENTION, THAT YOUR GOING THE WRONG WAY IN LIFE. OTHER TIMES IT CAN BE AN OUTSIDE FORCE TRYING TO DELAY YOU, TO DENY YOU AND EVEN TIMES TRY TO TAKE YOUR LIGHT OUT, OUT OF THIS LIFE, OUT OF THIS EARTH REALM. GOD HAS ALREADY SPOKEN LIFE OVER YOU, THAT NO WEAPON THAT IS FORMED AGAINST YOU, IT WILL NOT PROSPER.(ISAIAH 54:17). GOD'S WORD OVER YOU IS LOVE! " NOW WHEN I PASSED BY THEE, AND LOOKED UPON THEE, BEHOLD, THY TIME WAS THE TIME OF LOVE; AND I SPREAD MY SKIRT OVER THEE, AND COVERED THEY NAKEDNESS: YEA, I SWARE UNTO THEE, AND ENTERED INTO A COVENANT WITH THEE, SAITH THE LORD GOD, AND THOU BECAMEST MINE." (EZEKIEL 16:8).

YOU BECOMING A COVENANT WOMAN OR MAN OF GOD AND TO BE IN COVENANT WITH ALMIGHTY GOD IS NOTHING BUT AMAZING. FOR HIM TO PROMISE YOU WHAT HE WILL DO WHEN IT COMES TO YOU! WHAT HE WILL NOT SUFFER TO HAPPEN UNTO YOU BECAUSE OF HIS LOVE FOR YOU, BECAUSE OF WHO YOU ARE TO HIM. YOU BECOME PRECIOUS IN HIS EYES, THE APPLE OF HIS EYE. (DEUTERONOMY 32:10).

UTILIZING THIS POSITION THAT GOD HAS GRACIOUSLY GIVEN TO YOU, FOR YOUR ADVANTAGE; FOR EVERY AREA OF YOUR LIFE WILL GIVE YOU AN ADVANTAGE. UNDERSTANDING WHO YOU ARE AND WHO'S YOU ARE AS THE LORD WALKS WITH YOU ON THIS JOURNEY, HE WILL BEGIN TO PREPARE YOU AS A BRIDE OF CHRIST; PREPARING YOU FOR HIMSELF.

(STORY TIME)

AS I BEGAN WALKING WITH GOD, I USE TO HAVE DREAMS. THIS DREAM THE LORD GAVE ME, I WAS STANDING IN THIS WEDDING DRESS AND MY FIRST LADY, SHE WAS LIKE MAKING SURE MY DRESS WAS RIGHT. LIKE WHEN THE DESIGNER IS DESIGNING THE DRESS AND PINNING IT, BUT IT WAS LIKE SHE WAS MAKING SURE THERE WERE NO WRINKLES IN IT, MAKING SURE MY DRESS WAS PERFECT. I COULD FEEL IN THE DREAM THAT SHE WAS PREPARING ME AS A BRIDE FOR JESUS CHRIST. IT WAS LIKE I KNEW WHAT THIS DREAM MEANT. SHE WAS PUTTING THE FINISHING TOUCHES, MAKING SURE THERE WAS NO BLEMISH, NO WRINKLE AND NO SPOTS WERE ON MY DRESS.

I REMEMBER AS I WAS LOOKING AT THE MIRROR, THERE WAS SUCH BEAUTY THAT I KNEW IT WASN'T MY OWN. IT WASN'T ANY BEAT FROM A MAKEUP ARTIST BUT IT WAS THE BEAUTY OF THE LORD THAT WAS UPON ME. HE WILL PREPARE YOU UNTO HIM SELF. JUST ASK HIM FOR THE AREAS YOUR FALLING SHORT IN TO HELP YOU. ASK THE HOLY SPIRIT TO HELP YOU SPEEDILY, TIME IS WINDING UP AND WE MUST BE READY. WE MUST BE DILIGENT. FULFIL YOUR CALLING AND USE YOUR GIFTS FOR HIS GLORY. IF YOU DO NOT KNOW WHAT YOUR CALLING IS, PRAY AND ASK. I ASKED HOLY SPIRIT WHILE I WAS IN THE REST ROOM (IT USED TO BE WHERE I'D GO AND PRAY) EARLY IN MY WALK. I HEARD HIM CLEAR AS DAY TO ME WHAT MY CALLING WAS. WHEN JESUS WANTS YOU TO KNOW, HE WILL TELL YOU. THE SECRET THINGS BELONG TO HIM BUT THE THINGS THAT ARE REVEALED BELONG UNTO US.

(DEU 29:29)

HE WILL NOT ALLOW YOU TO BE BLINDSIDED NOR TAKEN BY SURPRISE. GOD WILL NOT REVEAL EVERYTHING UNTO YOU BUT HE WILL MAKE SURE THAT YOU ARE COVERED AND IT MAY NOT SURPRISE YOU BUT YOU MAY NOT KNOW EVERY SINGLE THING. YOUR PRAYER LIFE IS VERY IMPORTANT AND THE STRONGER AND FIRE THAT IT IS THE BETTER IT IS AND THE MORE INTIMATE IT IS WITH HOLY SPIRIT, HEAVEN WILL BE YOUR BACKING. THERE SHOULD BE SOME INTENSITY IN YOUR PRAYER LIFE, YOU WANT TO GET TO THAT PLACE THAT YOU LITERALLY CAN FEEL THE FIRE OF GOD IN YOU OR AND ON YOU AS YOU PRAYER. IF YOU DON'T PRAY AND TARRY THERE AND ASK THE LORD TO BE LIKE FIRE IN YOUR MOUTH, FIRE IN YOUR EYES AND FIRE IN YOUR BELLY. WE WANT TO BE BAPTIZED BY FIRE IN THE HOLY GHOST.

IF YOU DON'T KNOW HOW TO START OFF YOUR PRAYER, JUST GO INTO THANKSGIVING, YOU CAN NEVER GO WRONG THERE. THE LORD WILL SHIFT YOU WHEN HE'S READY TO MOVE YOU FROM THANKSGIVING INTO WORSHIP OR TO MAKE UP THE HEDGE AND STAND IN THE GAP FOR SOMEONE ELSE AS A INTERCESSOR. (EZEKIEL 22:30).

SO WE HAVE MOVED FROM SEEKING, TO THE IMPORTANCE OF ATMOSPHERE'S, TO PRAYER AND REPENTANCE. THIS CAN GO HONESTLY IN ANY ORDER. I WOULD LIKE FOR YOU TO TAKE A MOMENT TO TAKE IN ALL THAT HAS BEEN POURED OUT. ALL THAT HAS BEEN SHARED WITH YOU. TAKE THIS MOMENT IN PRAYER WITH YOUR THOUGHTS WITH GOD, TAKE A MOMENT TO PROCESS WHAT MAY BE GOING ON IN YOUR HEART AND IN YOUR MIND. WHAT YOU MAYBE HEARING WHAT THE LORD MAY SPEAK TO YOU.

WHEN ELI WAS TEACHING SAMUEL AND THE LORD STOOD AND CALLED FOR SAMUEL,
ELI TOLD SAMUEL "LIE DOWN: AND IT SHALL BE IF HE CALL THEE, THAT THOU SHALT SAY SPEAK LORD; FOR THY SERVANT HEARETH." (I SAMUEL 3:9). I AM NOT ELI, BUT I AM A SERVANT OF THE LORD, A DAUGHTER OF ZION. I WILL TELL YOU TO LISTEN TO THAT STILL SMALL VOICE THAT YOU MAY HEAR HIM SPEAKING TO YOU. BE STILL AND KNOW THAT HE IS GOD.

I WILL PRAY FOR YOU NOW

HEAVENLY FATHER GOD,

AS YOU HAVE GIVEN ME CHARGE TO COMPLETE THIS TASK, I PRAY FOR THEM, I PRAY THAT YOU WILL LEAD THEM AND GUIDE THEM INTO ALL TRUTH. I PRAY THAT YOUR HAND WOULD BE UPON THEM AND WOULD HOLD THEM. FOR THEY ARE YOURS AND I AM THINE. BE THOU GLORIFIED AND MAGNIFIED IN THEM FOR YOU HAVE THEM IN THE PALM OF YOUR HAND AND NOTHING CAN SNATCH THEM OUT OF IT. NOTHING CAN PLUCK THEM OUT OF YOUR HAND FATHER. I PRAY NOT THAT THOU SHOULDEST TAKE THEM OUT OF THE WORLD, BUT THAT YOU WILL KEEP THEM FROM EVIL. SANCTIFY THEM THROUGH YOUR WORD FOR YOUR WORD IS TRUTH. I PRAY FOR THEIR DESTINY, AND FOR THEIR PURPOSE THAT YOU HAVE CREATED THEM FOR IN THIS TIME AND SEASON.

HOLY SPIRIT I ASK THAT YOU WILL GIVE THEM EARS TO HEAR AND HEARTS TO OBEY YOU AT YOUR WORD. I PRAY AND I ASK FATHER GOD THAT YOU WOULD GIVE THEM WHAT THEY WILL NEED IN THIS HOUR TO PREVAIL AND OVER COME ANY OBSTACLES INTERFERING IN THEIR LIFE. I ASK THAT YOU WOULD CREATE A CLEAR PATH FOR THEM TO WALK, THAT WOULD MAKE EVERY CROOKED PATH STRAIGHT AND EVERY ROUGH PLACE PLAIN.

CALL FORTH THE WARRIOR IN THEM, THE INTERCESSOR IN THEM. WHATEVER YOU HAVE PLACED ON THE INSIDE OF THEM TO BE STIRRED LIKE NEVER BEFORE, THAT THE FIRE OF GOD IN THEM WOULD BE GREATER. THAT YOUR WORD WILL BE LIKE FIRE IN THEIR MOUTH, FIRE IN THEIR BELLY AND FIRE IN THEIR EYES. I PRAY THAT YOU WILL FILL THEIR CUP UNTIL IT OVER FLOWS WITH YOUR LOVE, WITH YOUR PEACE, WITH EVERY FRUIT OF THE SPIRIT THAT COMES WHEN YOU HAVE FILLED THEM WITH YOUR HOLY SPIRIT.

CULTIVATE WITHIN THEM HOW TO BE DISCIPLINED, HOW TO GET UNDER THEIR FLESH, TO DENY IT DAILY. HELP US LORD GOD TO LIVE IN YOUR WILL AND IN YOUR WAY. (I NOW INCLUDE MYSELF IN THIS PRAYER). FATHER GOD TO LIVE NOT ACCORDING TO THIS WORLD BUT ACCORDING TO YOUR WORD. WE ARE IN THIS WORLD BUT NOT OF IT. I THANK YOU LORD FOR WHAT YOUR GOING TO DO THROUGH US AND IN US. TAKE OUT THE STONY HEART AND GIVE US A HEART OF FLESH. A HEART THAT IS TENDER AND LOVING IN YOUR PRESENCE, IN YOUR SIGHT OH GOD, OUR LORD AND OUR REDEEMER. IT IS YOU THAT WE NEED, IT IS YOU THAT WE CAN'T LIVE WITHOUT. IT IS YOU OH GOD, THAT WE TURN OUR HEARTS TO, THAT WE TURN OUR EYES TOO. IT IS YOU OH GOD, IT IS YOU. HAVE YOUR WAY IN US OH GOD, HAVE THINE OWN WAY! IT IS IN YOU THAT WE LIVE, THAT WE MOVE AND THAT WE HAVE OUR BEING. LET US NEVER BE THE SAME.

IN JESUS MIGHTY NAME.

AMEN

TAKE THIS TIME TO WRITE OUT YOUR PRAYERS BEFORE THE LORD.

BEGIN TO JOURNAL….

TAKE THIS TIME TO WRITE OUT YOUR PRAYERS BEFORE THE LORD.

BEGIN TO JOURNAL….

TAKE THIS TIME TO WRITE OUT YOUR PRAYERS BEFORE THE LORD.

BEGIN TO JOURNAL....

TAKE THIS TIME TO WRITE OUT YOUR PRAYERS BEFORE THE LORD.

BEGIN TO JOURNAL….

SOMETIMES COMMITTING TO A VOW BEFORE THE LORD IS ANOTHER WAY TO GET TRACTION OR MOVEMENT ON THINGS THAT'S BEEN HARD TO MOVE OR TO SEE COME TO PASS IN YOUR LIFE....

ONE TIME I DID A VOW BEFORE THE LORD, I ASKED THE LORD FOR SOMETHING I REALLY NEEDED AND I MADE A VOW FOR AN AMOUNT I WANTED TO SOW AND BLESS THE KINGDOM OF GOD. I WAS YOUNG IN MY FAITH. I HAD MOVED AND SOME THINGS HAPPENED AND I FORGOT ABOUT THIS VOW, I WAS GOING THROUGH MY JOURNALS AND I SAW WHERE I HAD WROTE OUT THE VOW. I SAW THAT 2 YEARS HAD PAST AND I HAD NEVER COMPLETED THE VOW AND I REMEMBER GETTING SO SCARED!

INSTANTLY THE LORD SPOKE TO ME, AS LONG AS YOU COMPLETE IT. SO I MADE IT MY GOAL TO FINISH WHAT I HAD STARTED AND TO DO WHAT I VOWED UNTO THE LORD AND I DID EXACTLY WHAT I VOWED TO GOD. YOU HAVE TO COMPLETE AND DO WHAT YOU PROMISED. DON'T MAKE A VOW AND DO NOT PAY IT. PRAY IT OUT, MAKE SURE YOU ARE READY TO STICK TO IT AND COMPLETE IT, BECAUSE GOD IS FAITHFUL AND WILL DO HIS PART. HE WILL DO IT BEFORE YOU EVEN COMPLETE YOUR VOW. THEREFORE YOU MUST BE DILIGENT TO COMPLETE IT.

FINISH WRITING OUT YOUR PRAYERS AND OR YOUR VOWS TO GOD.... BE FAITHFUL, BE DILIGENT.

I PRAY THIS BOOK HAS SPARKED A PASSION AND A LOVE FOR GOD LIKE NEVER BEFORE. I PRAY THAT THIS BOOK WILL CAUSE YOU TO LOOK TO THE HILLS FROM WHENCE COMES YOUR HELP, FOR YOUR HELP COMES FROM THE LORD. THIS BOOK WAS MEANT TO BE SHORT, SHARP AND POWERFUL. WHAT HAS ALWAYS HELPED ME IN MY WALK IN GOD WAS BRINGING MYSELF INTO REMEMBRANCE OF THE ENCOUNTERS THAT I HAVE HAD WITH GOD AND WHAT HE HAS DONE FOR ME. REMINDING MYSELF THAT GOD IS ALWAYS WITH ME AND HE WILL NEVER LEAVE ME NOR FORSAKE ME. WITHER YOU HAVE THESE ENCOUNTERS WITH GOD OR NOT, JUST KNOW THAT YOU CAN DO ALL THINGS THROUGH CHRIST THAT STRENGTHENS YOU. SPEND SOME TIME NOW WITH HIM, TURNING YOUR HEART TO HIM. LAY ASIDE THE WEIGHT AND THE SIN THAT SO EASILY BESETS YOU. LAY IT ALL DOWN, FOR ONLY WHAT YOU DO FOR CHRIST WILL LAST.

AMEN.

PAGE 36

Made in the USA
Columbia, SC
07 May 2024